The
Lamb's Crossing

Regarding Community

Jane P. Butler

The Lamb's Crossing

Regarding Community

Copyright © 2012 by Jane P. Butler

ISBN-13: 978-1469996691
ISBN-10: 1469996693

This book is written in Times Roman Font.
All drawings were illustrated by Jane P. Butler.

Dedicated to To Lauren and Sabrina Velegol

Beloved grandchildren
Loved Unconditionally
And always in my heart
To stay.

My prayer is that each will find the heart to lead others
and in doing so will find God leading them.

Contents

Preface

This story is an allegory that was first begun thirty years ago. It began as a children's picture story about a little lamb that wanted to help her friends cross over the bridge to the new land.

As my career moved from teaching to administration, the audience expanded to include adults. What began as a story of friendship, turned into an autobiography. My teaching career began in Schenectady, New York. After I married, I taught in Moorestown, New Jersey and after my daughter was born, taught in Medford, New Jersey. Wherever the place, I always found friends because we shared a common goal: teaching children. I will long remember the sharing, the laughter, and the feeling of being a part of a greater whole. I was asked to become an assistant principal in the school where I was teaching. My friendships changed. The first day as an administrator changed me. When the students poured into the school and walked past me into their classrooms, I had no place to go except my small office with a sign reading assistant principal. I had to establish a community of teachers who added leadership to the common goal of educating children. It was a different mindset: one of consensus and collaboration. A person had to get things done, establish community so that children benefitted. After 15 years of being a principal in Riverside, New Jersey, a 'monster' with a top down philosophy chose to lead by bullying. That was the battle. Out of this story came this one.

The hope is that whoever reads this story, will learn what it takes to be a leader. I pray the reader focuses on the 'heart' of the story; the unconditional love Lamb has for the other animals, the fear in the hearts of those who know they must cross the bridge but just can't handle the invisible force that controls their lives preventing them from saving each animal family's life.

The Lamb's Crossing

Regarding Community

Jane P. Butler

The Lamb's Crossing

The land was changing. Cracks could be seen in the dried mud where animals usually gathered to quench their thirst. There was no promise of water for the future. Drought was a constant. The waterfall that once gushed over the edge was now one narrow line pointing to the rocks below. Last year the fish struggled upstream. This year there was only the stench.

In the midst of the drought in one small meadow can be seen an invasion of moving iron monsters scraping the ground and mechanical shovels digging into the land. The sloping meadow was being leveled.

In the midst of this disappearing meadow lived Lamb. The machines came one morning surprising Lamb with the noise of an army invasion.

Lamb began to worry about what the machines would do to her beautiful space. Even if she didn't want to move, she would have to. She would have to move across the bridge; leave the past behind and begin once again. The land across the river was a land that had not been touched. She would have to find a new place there.

As she moved toward the bridge she soon learned that there was an even greater problem. You could not see it or touch it or feel or hear it. There was some invisible force keeping the animals from crossing over. It was as if a wall had been built and yet there was no such thing. Lamb had never encountered anything like this. This was especially frustrating because of her vision to cross the bridge to the new land with her friends. This was her answer to the problem with the land. Together, they would explore and stand in awe of what they would find before them. Her dream was full of pictures of birds of every color. She imagined reptiles and amphibians of every species living in peace. All living things

4

would live in harmony with the land. Beauty would be seen everywhere just as the land on this side of the bridge had been beautiful at one time. How easy it would be to walk the bridge to the other side!

At first, crossing the bridge had not been an issue. Lamb had no doubt that the pilgrimage to the other side would happen. The animals were already moving toward the bridge.

Coming to the Bridge

Down by the edge of the bridge, an invisible force became the gatekeeper. It had a sense of territory and power.

The animals, oblivious to the blockade, went to the bridge to look across to the new land. The first to arrive at the gate was rabbit.

Skittish, Rabbit hopped toward the edge of the bank.

A voice was heard. "STOP, THINK! BE SURE!" Rabbit, ready to sprint away, stared at the bridge.

"Why do you want to cross the bridge?" Rabbit thinks he hears.

"I want to gaze at the land of the future," replied Rabbit.

"How do you know it is what you want? Better to be safe than sorry, I always say. Who knows, you may have to work harder than you ever have! Going to a new place will mean finding a new dwelling place as well as a supply of food. Who knows what enemies you will encounter?"

"But it looks so beautiful."

"Are you sure?"

Rabbit, who was not accustomed to such thinking, decided not to look any further but to go back to his safe home in the meadow. He had much to think about before he would cross the bridge.

The Force was pleased. It waited for their next encounter.

Bear was big, burly and gruff in his ways. As he began to cross, he felt something. As he began to cross, he filled his great volumes of air as if to appear louder, angrier and more powerful than he really was. He was not accustomed to dealing with an invisible enemy.

"Let me pass", the bear roared.
Seeing no one, bear became angry.

"Show yourself!" yelled Bear. Still no one showed.

Having no one to fight, the Bear returned to his cave to think of the next move.

The force had won.

By this time, other animals had heard that it wasn't so easy to cross the bridge and began to question its importance. Strange that no one thought about what force had a right to stop everyone. Most preferred to remain where life felt certain and comfortable.

One animal more, adventurous, became curious. That animal was Pony. Who could have such power to keep him from crossing? In his young and frisky style, he decided to attempt to cross to the new world. As he approached the bridge, he was a bit apprehensive having heard of the invisible something.

"Are you really ready to cross the bridge?" Pony heard a voice.

Confused, Pony said," Who are you?"

No answer.

"What do you have to tell me? That the other side is a terrible place to be? That it is not worth it? Stay in the present where you will know what is before you?"

 "But what about the adventure of it all? What about the future?"
"What about the responsibility to your family?"

Pony was now frustrated. He had heard nothing but his own voice.

The pony may have been young and full of adventure, but he also knew the responsibility to his family. He decided to go back and think some more.

Now these animals were not prone to remain quiet. Lamb had always encouraged discussion. Something had happened to Rabbit, Bear and Pony. Each seemed to lack the confidence they once had. Something in each animal's eyes alarmed Lamb and the others.

Lamb knew that these three had not crossed the bridge and she sensed this had something to do with that 'look' each had.

Lamb decided one day to invite the three to lunch to see if he could discover what was troubling them. The morning of the lunch, Lamb arose early and went to the bridge to see what was happening?

Lamb thought she heard "Wait! Stop! Think a little!"
She took time to look around. There was no visible sign of anyone.

How can someone deal with something that she can't confront? It's there. You can't see it or really hear it? How do you discern what it is?

Lamb had no intention of allowing anything from keeping her friends from crossing the bridge. She decided to have lunch with her friends.

The Discussion

Lunch with Rabbit, Bear and Pony was quiet. Each one was waiting for the other to begin. Lamb, sensing their discomfort, began.

"You know, I was down at the bridge this morning and a strange thing happened to me. I could swear that there was someone preventing me from crossing the bridge and yet there was no one.

"Did you cross the bridge?" asked Rabbit.

"No"

"Well, said Rabbit, I have to admit, I was kept from crossing but not because of hard work or long hours but because of risk to my family."

"Are you afraid?" queried Lamb.

"I wasn't afraid!" boasted Bear. I stepped up to and told them I would pass if I so desired or something like that! I know I was very angry!"

"Tell me more" encouraged Lamb.

"There's not much more to say. How do you fight something that is not there?"

"Did you cross then?"

"I did not, but I will the next time," boasted Bear.

"Were you afraid?" Lamb asked again.

"Bears aren't supposed to be afraid", answered Bear.

12

"I know but"

"Why is it so important to cross over anyway?" asked Bear defensively.

Before Lamb could answer, Pony spoke. "Well, I was met with questions that came from nowhere. I decided to wait because I felt no one would want to go to a land with more problems than we have right here. Besides, I have a family. I have responsibilities."

She summarized the feelings of the three. "It sounds like this force has convinced each of us not to cross the bridge. There's some fear of the unknown, some hesitation because of the change that might take place. I think the force has done a wonderful job of keeping us from the bridge."

Rabbit, Pony and Bear all agreed that each had been prevented from crossing the bridge. They were also relieved that Lamb understood the problem at the bridge.
Before leaving, Bear could not resist saying, "Just give me the word and we will cross the bridge by force."

Pony responded, "I don't know. Is it really worth the fight?"

Rabbit remained quiet.

The Eye of the Eagle

Her first task was to meet with Eagle for she needed the sharp eyes of this magnificent bird. It wasn't difficult to find him since there was only one mountain. Lamb knew she would find him at the top of the old oak tree.

"Well, hello friend. This must be an important visit. I have watched you climb with no rest. Let me fly near you," said Eagle.

"How's the world from up there?" asked Lamb.

"To tell you the truth, it looks a bit crowded. It has become a little more difficult to find food since the forest fire last year. People are tearing down the forest in order to build homes. The drought last year left the remaining land cracked and dry. The river seems to dry up earlier and earlier every year as does the lakes and ponds. To tell you the truth, I see more death, more struggles and more fear in the eyes of my friends."

Lamb responded, "I see the same."

"Eagle, I have come to ask you a favor."

"If it is in my power", replied Eagle.

"Fly to the land across the river and see if it's crowded. See for yourself what lies there."

Eagle answered, "I will go tomorrow and report my findings to you. Is that all?"

"Not exactly" said Lamb.

"Somehow, I thought there was more to this!"

"Would you be willing to speak to our friends about what you see?" asked Lamb.

"You know I am more of an observer. I will think about your request," answered Eagle.

Continuing Lamb inquired, "When can I see you again?"

"Tomorrow; early" answered Eagle.

"Well, Eagle, I had better head down the mountain before dark. Thanks for your help."

Eagle knew this must be an important job because Lamb was not one to ask. He was determined to bring back whatever he could in order to please Lamb.

He began his journey even though night was upon him. After flying over the vast land beyond the bridge, Eagle realized that there would be much to report. He realized that there was more than one place for an Eagle to build a nest for there were many mountains for as far as one could see. There appeared to be fewer animals. Knowing the land mass was far more expansive, Eagle concluded that the number of animals were the same. Not only was there enough food, there seemed to be a greater variety. He began to wonder why he had not soared over this new world.

Suddenly, Eagle was filled with such excitement he wanted to tell everyone especially Lamb. And so he did.

It was about twilight when Lamb spotted Eagle coming toward him. After giving Eagle a warm welcome, she invited Eagle to stay. (Obviously, Lamb was curious).

"Tell me" said Lamb.

Eagle could hardly speak slowly enough to be understood. The wonders of the new world were spectacular! The vast expanse of green fields filled with little animals for eagles to eat, the forests filled with places for eagles to perch; the clear lakes, ponds and streams filled with fish for the eagle to eat.

Although the Eagle's description was a bit self-centered, the vision of the other side was very exciting. Lamb wanted to cross to the new land.
And she wanted to cross with her family and friends.

Lamb asked again, "Will you speak to the group?"

"Yes, yes, yes!" shouted Eagle.

And so the community gathered and listened to the Eagle. His enthusiasm caught everyone. Questions were asked and answered. Rabbit reasoned that the group must cross to the new land. Pony couldn't understand how he had allowed the force to keep him from such an opportunity for his family. Bear was ready to storm the gates in heroic style and move on to the Promised Land.

"Let's go!" they all shouted.

The Decision

The report from the Eagle was enough to energize the group. What was the next step? That is what Lamb was pondering as she sat quietly listening to the enthusiasm of the group. Lamb knew what happens to enthusiasm. All too quickly it turns to doubt. She needed to find time to think. She drew away from her friends and went to the meadow. This was the place where she could relax and come up with a plan for overcoming the doubt that was sure to come. She couldn't help but think that the meadow would soon be gone. "How can I instill courage in the hearts of my friends? How can I get the force to allow anyone to cross the bridge?"

She felt that she would have to answer all of the questions the animals asked. She would share her thoughts and ask for more ideas, building a community of strength rather than everyone relying on her. Her strength would have to flow to the others. But how?

It seemed so unfair that bullies like the force could affect such power. Where did it come from? How did they keep it? What power allows them to occupy the bridge? Lamb knew these questions must be answered before any decisions could be made.

Further, the question is how the community comes to allow the bullies to have such power. What is it within each of them? What was it that made each to be so filled with fear?

Lamb knew the power of fear. It would be easier to engage in combat than to deal with the fear inside this community. It is a bully itself. It waits for the weakest moment and jumps into action causing the adrenalin to begin before the thought reaches the brain. It causes actions that cover up the true person's character. Yes, fear was the biggest enemy. Lamb had found the enemy and it wasn't at the bridge.

But, alas, understanding fear did not give Lamb a clue of what to do. She would have to use all of her critical thinking skills. She went again to her favorite meadow, stood and looked over the valley as if the view would give her the answer. It did. She saw something down by the river that gave her what would be the beginning of an answer. She saw her friend, the beaver. Of course, that's it!

The Gift

The Lamb could hardly wait to reach her friend, Beaver. She noticed that her friend was biting into the tree trunk of a tree near the edge of the river.

Lamb came closer and yelled, "Hey, Beaver! It's me, Lamb. You are doing a mighty fine job of cutting down that tree! You have chewed that trunk to a point where it has to fall!"

"Watch out, Lamb! I never know which way the tree will fall. I want this one to fall over the river," shouted Beaver. Just as the words were spoken, the tree began to creak and then fall right into the river.

"Great job, Beav," encouraged Lamb.

"Thanks," said Beaver. What brings you to the river? I heard you were up in the mountain with Eagle.

"Actually, you do!" said Lamb. I was trying to resolve a serious problem so I came to the meadow to look for guidance. When I looked down at the river, I saw you and an answer came. No details yet!

"Yeah, right!" answered Beaver. Little me whose reason for being is to chop down trees and build dams? I am the wonder animal; the guru of the land?"

Lamb explained, "Sometimes those who know their gifts and steadfastly and quietly use them are the wisest of all."

"Lamb, you have this knack of making me feel so important. You are indeed a good friend. I think that is your gift," replied Beaver.

"Well, we are going to need each of the animal's gifts to resolve the problem," answered Lamb.

"Please tell me! What are you talking about? I have no idea."

Lamb explained the events of the last three days. That there was this unseen force that had come to their land. It was staying down by the old bridge near the oak tree. Each time someone came to the bridge, the force had persuaded each to not cross. They used reason with the Rabbit, fear with Pony and intimidation with Bear. Lamb told Beaver that she hated to see her friends afraid. Something had to be done. She told Beaver that there were two problems. One was dealing with fear, reason, and intimidation. These negatives must be erased before they encircle the land and immobilize his friends leaving no one with any courage to move on to new beginnings.

"Speaking of new beginnings," continued Lamb. There is a second problem that needs to be resolved. There are problems with the land we have loved for so long.

"Tell me about it!" interrupted Beaver. Beaver already knew of the problem with the land. "The tree is falling over a stream of mud. How can I make a dam when there is not enough water flowing? A day's work does not satisfy; anymore. What are we going to do?"

"We had better decide soon, said Lamb. Have you been to the land on the other side?"

"No, I have been too busy, said Beaver. I haven't considered moving but maybe I should."

"Would you be willing to meet with some of the other animals? I want to form a committee."

"Í am busy but I have to admit the problem will take more than hard, physical work. I'm in."

"Thanks so much! I'll let you know!"

Lamb was beginning to feel anxious. There was a feeling of urgency and fear welling up inside. Wasn't that the same invisible force that kept her friends from crossing?

The Committee

Lamb knew all about committees. Some were successful and others were disasters. She knew it only took one animal having a difficult day to ruin a meeting. Hopefully, all would see the crisis as serious enough to put personal feelings aside.

Who to ask? Beaver had already agreed. He would be the practical one. Pony, Bear, Rabbit and Eagle were aware of the issue. They would need to be included. That would be five. It was enough.

And so Lamb, Beaver, Rabbit, Bear, Pony and Eagle all gathered in the meadow for a most important meeting; one that might change their lives.

Knowing the importance of the meeting, each animal wanted to influence the outcome. Lamb wanted everyone to agree to cross the bridge to the new land. She also wanted to deal with the invisible force.

Beaver wanted to detail the work to be done. He wanted everyone to storm the bridge with him as the general in charge. Rabbit saw himself sitting quietly listening and speaking. Pony was in a hurry because he had to get back home to his family for a picnic. They were all impatient.

The meeting was doomed before it began. Here's what happened.

Lamb began, "We are here today to resolve two problems; whether to cross the bridge to the new land or stay here. If we do, how do we overcome the force?
"What do you mean? If I wanted to cross the bridge, I would. Let's all storm the bridge together", exclaimed Bear.

"What is this invisible force?" asked Rabbit.

"Who cares?" said Bear who was rearing up on his hind legs. "Cross!"

Now he was getting everyone riled. Lamb said, "Bear, you are acting truly courageous! We hear you loud and clear. Let's hear what the others have to say."

Pony stomped, "How long is this going to take? I have family waiting."

Eagle pointed out that he was THE SOURCE of information.

Rabbit sat and listened in dismay.

Poor Lamb! She was attempting to help and everyone was pulling the process in a different direction.

Committees usually do not work and this one was no exception. Lamb had lost total control of the situation. She needed to withdraw to the meadow and think. She should have asked Owl to be part of the committee. Too late now. Maybe he saw something.

She eyed Owl perched in the tree.

"Lamb that was some meeting. I saw you being pulled into so many different directions. It was a sad sight!"

"I felt so useless! I wanted to bring my friends to the new land. Each wanted something else. Bear said he wanted to cross. What could I do?" cried Lamb.

"Think about what you just said. I want. I want. Bear wants. Pony wants. How can you get everyone to go in the same direction? Your answer is in the power of persuasion. You have to decide that your idea is worth consideration. That's only the first step. Devising a plan will be the next step. You will need to gather some facts and examples that will convince the group.

"But how will I get their attention?"

"Now there's the challenge!" said Owl. I only observe. Creative beginnings are not my style.

Lamb went back to the meadow saying, "What can I do?"

Lamb was forlorn. As she saw her family, she thought how easy it is to be with one's own kind. There is such a safe feeling. Lamb wanted to share her feelings. She began to cry. The lambs surrounded her ready to listen.

Lamb told them of her feelings of helplessness. She felt so accepted in the circle of family. She began to tell her story. The family listened with concern. Although no solutions were forthcoming, Lamb was thankful for their support. It felt so good!

Lamb's disappointment was that everyone was only thinking of one solution. It was a far cry from the feeling of sharing she felt from family. That's what she needed. Lamb knew what she thought was best for all but she didn't know how to get there. After realizing the situation, she somehow felt better.

Slowly some ideas began to germinate in her newly cleared mind. She thought back to the Owl's advice. You need facts and examples. Maybe in her rush to find an answer, she had forgotten that the group needed to be involved in the decision making process.

There was no solution forthcoming. She wasn't even sure that her solution of crossing the river to the new land was a good one.

One thing she did know. The group had some work to do.

Now, how do I get the group back to a committee meeting after the fiasco of the last meeting? It wasn't going to be easy.

It would take a miracle.

Reflection Pool

Lamb had always been reflective. The meadow was the place where she could go, feel safe and reflect. Just the thought of going to her special place calmed her fear. As she walked toward the meadow her thoughts were on identifying the problem. She knew she couldn't rely on a miracle. This would not take a miracle. It would take a process. That led Lamb back to the beginning. How do you get the group to even meet to discuss the process for solving the problem?

As she reached the meadow she became concerned about the meadow. Not only was the grass scorched, brown; burnt from the months of grueling sunrays beaming on the hill.; the bulldozers were beginning to thrust the meadow dirt into huge piles. An urgent feeling came over her. Now it was affecting her and the family of lambs. A feeling that she was self-centered made her feel guilty. She moved her thoughts toward the entire community. It suddenly dawned on her! Maybe that was the problem. She wasn't listening. Her solution was not the only answer.

She had found the enemy. It was within herself. She began to think about what the others had said. She soon realized that she hadn't listened that carefully. She could only remember what she had thought about each of the animals when they spoke. She couldn't remember what each had said. Next time she would make an effort to listen.

The problem was how to make "next time" a reality.

Slithering Solutions

Lamb was deep in thought when suddenly there was a movement in the grass. She jumped, turned and saw snake pass between her feet.

"Why do you have to sneak around so? You scared the living daylights out of me. I hate when you do that?"

"That's why I do it!" said Snake.

"Well don't do it again! I mean it!" Lamb said annoyed at the snake.

"You know I am a bit perturbed with you also", complained Snake.

"What are you talking about?"

"I am talking about not being invited to the meeting. From what I hear it wasn't that big of a deal anyway. Everyone was upset with you."

"With me? What have you heard?" Lamb's thoughts were racing. The first reaction was one of anger. After all, had not she been the one who was trying to solve the problem? Wasn't she the one who called the meeting? What did everyone else do except whine and moan?"

She kept silent merely because her anger was so great she couldn't think of what to say.

Snake continued. "The group thinks that you came with the solution. You proceeded to ram it down their throats. Their reactions were in answer to your closed mind." Of course, the snake loved telling Lamb that she wasn't so smart after all.

Snake thought, "I hope she is very upset. That's what she gets for not inviting me."

Lamb was fighting her own negative thoughts. She began to feel responsible for the dilemma. One part of her knew she was not responsible for the condition of the land: the other blamed those who caused the land to change. She had to make some decisions before she could meet with the group. She had to be more prepared this time. Owl, Eagle, Beaver, and even Snake had talked to her and she was grateful for their advice and information. Now she knew that she would have to do some tall thinking. And she did. She went to the meadow. This time there was no family; just Lamb. She was thankful that the family was nowhere to be seen. This time she did not need consoling. She needed to stay quiet and wait. Whatever she decided, she wanted to remember that this was a decision for everyone to make. Somehow this was a relief. The burden of responsibility was somewhat lifted. What she needed to do was to find some way to bring everyone back to the committee. There needed to be some way to melt all of these ideas into one decision.

Before the meeting, Lamb would have to meet with each individually. She would have to admit her shortcomings and ask for new beginnings. Just the knowledge of the process of what to do gave her courage. Strange how that happens! When Lamb faced her biggest enemy; her own personal war with herself, the answers came. Be humble; admit the wrong and begin again. A new energy filled her and she was eager to begin.

The Longest Journey

The longest journey is that of change. Lamb was about to begin change that would affect each animal. The word of the day would be SLOW. Go slowly, be patient. Knowing this, Lamb felt a calm she had not experienced for a long time. She first approached Snake. It wasn't difficult to find him. The leaves were wavering as snake moved through the grass.

"I see you snake! What's happening?"

"Well, I have been trying to find some food to eat like a frog or a rodent. There is none to be found."

"Why not?

"The bulldozers are destroying homes and filling in the ponds. Rodents and frogs are dying."

"What do you think can be done?"

"Good question. We don't have much to say about what humans do. I have already moved steadily toward the creek."

"So you have seen this problem coming?" asked Lamb.

"Not at first but lately I have been alarmed at times when I see dead animals in my path."

"Yes, that's exactly what I am saying."

"What are your plans?

"I honestly don't know."

"What do you think about the possibility of passing over to the land beyond the river?" queried Lamb.

"Are there construction workers there?"

"You know when I talked to Eagle, I never asked that question. I could ask him if you would like," offered Lamb.

"We could go together," answered Snake.

"I would like that very much," replied Lamb. And off they went, the Snake and the Lamb.

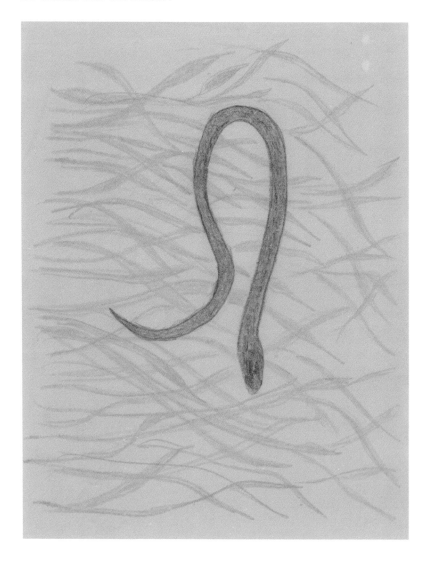

As they came near to the bridge, Lamb told Snake that whatever was to happen, she would be right beside him. The invisible force seemed to be just that; when they admitted the obstacle; it disappeared. Even so, they approached slowly. Crossing the bridge together; one walking; the other wiggling its body forward, the two felt somewhat like adventurers. With that spirit, they stepped and projected forward onto the new land. They felt somewhat like when they were little. They wanted to cross over and do it again! There was this feeling of victory and exhilaration. Lamb looked down at snake and if they could have given each other a high five as they had seen humans do, they would have.

"I think I will stay here."

Lamb thought, "One has crossed; surely the others will come."

As she turned back to the bridge, she couldn't help but be pleased that the first hurdle had been successfully taken.

Who would be the next? She did not have to wait too long. Eagle was flying back from his daily flights to the new land. She wouldn't have to convince him. That made three who had crossed. This only helped Lamb to feel positive once again.

As Lamb crossed, he spied Beaver chewing furiously just down from the bridge.

"Beaver"

"Lamb, did I see you crossing the bridge?"

"You sure did! Snake is there now. Would you like to cross with me?"

"Why would I cross over the bridge when I can cross over the log that is about to fall over the creek?" replied Beaver.

"You have a point! Can I use the log also?," asked Lamb.

"Wouldn't it be easier for you to use the bridge?"

"Maybe so, but I wanted to go the way you go," answered Lamb.

Suit yourself!

"Will you help me across?" queried Lamb.

"I will make the log as safe as possible."

"Thanks."

And with that, Lamb and Beaver crossed the creek using a different way.

When Beaver got to the other side, he turned to Lamb.

"What's the difference?" The creek is still drying up.

Lamb pondered. "Do you think there might be some other source of water somewhere?"

"I don't know!"

"Shall we take a look?"

"Ok, but I must get back to my work as soon as possible."

"If we see Eagle, we will have to ask him. What do you think?"

"I like that idea."

"Would you like me to speak to Eagle and you can continue working?"

"I would like that! Thanks!"

"Beaver, would you mind if some of the animals used the log to cross?"

"Is that what you meant when you said I was an answer to the problem?"

"I did not know it at the time, but yes!"

"On second thought, said Beaver, I think I will explore a bit before I come back."

"Great!" said Lamb.

Eagle, Snake, Beaver and Lamb. This was a good morning's work. Lamb decided to celebrate and spend some time reflecting before continuing.

As she thought about what had happened so quickly, she realized how much fun it was to be a listener and an encourager. She loved the idea of asking Eagle on behalf of Beaver. She also realized that she had now created opportunities for Beaver, Snake, Eagle or Beaver to meet with some animal in the community and guide them to the new land. Is this how it is with change: one little step at a time; each family making their own decision? Somehow she felt closer to her friends: perhaps because she saw them as individuals and not subjects to be led. What a day this had been!

Lamb was thinking that this was a bit too easy! She had moved from feeling frustrated to ecstatic. Beware! At least that is what her heart was telling her. Regardless, she moved forward to speak with Rabbit.

She came upon Rabbit and his family as they scurried through the trees looking for food.

"Good morning, Rabbit family" said Lamb.

"Good morning, Lamb. How are you? We are on our way to look for our lunch.

"Are you having any luck?"

"Sh, I don't want the family to know how difficult it is. They think we are playing a game."

"What would you think about trying to find food on the other side?"

"Don't start with the bridge. I don't know which scares me more, that voice at the bridge or the amount of time I search for food each day."

"Suppose I tell you that there is another way to cross over? You could just as easily cross back over." asked Lamb.

"What?"

"Beaver has felled a tree and he has scurried across the tree to the other side. He is there now exploring."

"I will go only if I am not bullied by the voice."
"What if I were to tell you that voice is your own fear speaking to you?" asked Lamb.

"Don't confuse me. I don't understand what you are saying."

"I am sorry. What if I go with you to the log and see if the voice speaks."

"Just me. My family will wait here. I don't want anything to happen to them."

"You sound a bit like Pony" I can understand your concern. Let's take a walk to the log?"

"Ok". After telling his family where he was going, Lamb and Rabbit traveled to the log.

On their way, they met Pony running through the meadow with his family. Rabbit said, "Pony, would you like to go with us to Beaver's log. We are sidestepping the bridge and crossing over the log in order to avoid the voice."

Lamb stayed silent and kept her philosophy quiet.

"I can't cross over a log. I will slip and break my leg. I will need to use the bridge."

"Would you like to come with us and watch us crossing? Then we could hail you if there is any problem or we could shout back our victory."

"I would be happy to help in any way."

The log was certainly no problem for Rabbit. Lamb remembered that it was a bit difficult but had made it once and was ready to try again. After crossing, Rabbit noticed how green the land was and though that he needed to explore to look for food and a place to live. He decided to stay. Lamb walked back and spoke to Pony.

"Pony, Beaver, Snake, Owl, and now Rabbit have all crossed the bridge and have stayed to explore. What would you like to do?"
"I will have to use the bridge."

"This stream is very shallow. You could just gallop over."

"I will discuss it with my family."

"OK" See you soon!

Lamb began thinking that perhaps she should find her own family and lead them across. Her family knew of the plans to cross the bridge. Were they ready to cross the bridge or swim across? That was to be seen. Lamb was sure that they would be no problem.

As she came upon the meadow, she noticed that the flock was all gathered as if a discussion was taking place.

"Hey, everyone! What's up?"

"How come we are the last to go across the river?" You've discussed with everyone else going to the new land. Not your own family. We saw you taking Beaver, Snake, and Rabbit. Eagle was influenced by you to go to the new land. What about us?"

Lamb felt guilty and defensive at the same time. She knew they would not listen if she was either of the above. She decided to apologize and try to move to a decision about crossing.

"You are right!" I love you and I want you to cross the river as well. I came to you when I was upset and yet ignored you when trying to help you make a decision to cross the river. Please accept my apology."

"We love you also. It's just that we wanted to be included in this exciting adventure."

"Then it's decided? We will cross the bridge to the new land?"

"Some of us will. Others will stay and wait for news of the other side. You haven't entirely convinced us."

"May I help those going across?"

"We hear there are two choices: the log or the bridge?"

"Yes. Which shall it be?"

"The bridge."

"Now what about this force; this voice? How shall we handle it?"

"I am betting that there will not be a voice; force. I think that enough animals have crossed. The force has lost its power."

"How will we know?"

"We will have to go the bridge?"

"Let's go. We would like you to go first."

"I will," said Lamb. Off they went to the bridge. Would the fact that there was some hesitancy and anxiety give the force power? That was yet to be seen.

Having some of her friends already on the other side, gave Lamb courage. She approached the bridge with an assertive gait. She heard nothing and began walking across the bridge.

"Wait! I heard something," said a lamb.

Lamb said, "I want you to take the first step toward me. Focus on me and walk right past that force and feel victory."

After some hesitation, they walked quickly onto the bridge. The force field was gone. Lamb was especially filled with joy for this was her family. There was much celebration! The lambs could not wait to explore just as the others. Lamb asked one other lamb to come back with her to tell the others and bring them across.

As the rest of the Lamb family was crossing, Pony was seen pausing at the bridge. He hesitated and then galloped away toward his family. The force was still lurking.

Lamb knew that this was the right time to stay with her family and join the exploration of the new land. She had learned much during this time of change. Leaders lead. They don't fix. Leaders listen and assist the community to make decisions on their own. Leaders facilitate. They don't dictate.

As she looked across the bridge, she could just see the chimney of a new house being built. Someday, the animals might have to move to yet another place. This time they would be ready. The question that will stay with Lamb is, "Will there be another land to turn to?"

That's another story.

Ole' Turtle

Ole' Turtle was watching the activity at the edge of the stream by the bridge. She sat in a perfect place. She remembered clearly the first time she watched Lamb come to the bridge. And then Pony, Rabbit, and Bear came. Each stopped at the bridge. Lamb showed no response. Pony galloped away. Rabbit ran. Bear bristled as he moved from the bridge. It was as if each saw something.

Turtle did not see or hear anything that would prevent her friends from going over the bridge. One day she saw Eagle fly across to the new land and she wondered why she hadn't stopped as she passed over the bridge. It was all so confusing. Snake crossed with Lamb, then Rabbit, Pony and finally all of Lamb's family. Who was left behind? How did Lamb persuade her friends to cross the bridge? Surely, it was her leadership.

Turtle realized she was the one left behind. The exodus had begun. The people had won. Was the people's progress the animals' destruction? She had to give Lamb credit for leading the others to a better place. Her leadership walked animals over the bridge. She could envision her continuing her influence in the new place across the river. Would she cross again to lead others? That was yet to be seen.

Curiosity moved Turtle to the bridge. She moved slowly observing carefully in order to find what had caused the animals to hesitate. Or was it gone? As she ambled, she saw the stones imbedded in the mud in the creek. There were some darker spots where some moisture could be seen. There were also deep cracks. There certainly was no water flowing under the bridge. The banks had a crisp sound under her feet. She had not realized the severity of the drought. And then her wise mind shifted to the progress just behind her. Was it manmade drought or people caused drought? Regardless, the animal kingdom suffered. Moving closer to the bridge, Turtle prepared for what was to come. Nothing came. Whatever was there no longer existed; at least not for Turtle. She ventured across the bridge. Slowly, she set her eyes for the other side. As she reached the center, she looked to the new land. It was as crispy on the edges just as the other side. What was it that brought Lamb? She needed to look further. She knew she would have to spend at least one night on the other side. Going slowly meant there would be no opportunity to cross back until the morning. As she reached the other side, she saw Lamb watching her.

"Lamb, how are you?"

"Turtle, it so good to see you," said Lamb.

"Lamb, I have watched from the knoll. What was that about? Rabbit, Pony, Bear, and you stopped at the bridge. I just finished crossing with no problem."

"Turtle, that something was fear. Each reacted differently. Believe me, the reason was the same. Fear filled them. At first, I persuaded them to meet to discuss why we had not crossed the bridge. Eagle had gone earlier and found green grass and trees and no people. That meeting did not go well. Eagle acted like he was the expert. Pony was in a hurry to get home. Rabbit did not know what to think. Bear was defiant. I realized I was not listening. Rather I was set on the goal of crossing the bridge. Each reacted and the entire meeting was a disaster. Of course there were many other animals. They had not been invited and were quick to tell me all of my shortcomings. Some were upset that they had not been invited!

I went to the meadow to think. That's when you saw me bring each animal across separately. It was very successful. Finally, I brought my family across."

"And what have you found?" asked Turtle.

"Not exactly a paradise but so much better than where we were."

"What will we do about those who are still in danger?"

"All are welcome to come to this side. Now that you know what I have told you, you can go back and tell those on the other side to join us."

"What about those who are weak and will not be able to cross the bridge, or walk across the creek bed? Who will help them?"

"I don't know. I hadn't thought about it," said Lamb.

A tear came from Turtle. Isn't that the way it is? Those who are able can conquer their fear, cross the bridge on their own and start a new life. Others perhaps have a greater fear, can't cross the bridge easily and believe that they are left behind to fend for themselves. Who will be their leader?

Lamb felt a pain in her heart. She thought she loved all in the kingdom. Why had she forgotten those less able? She had spent the last few days feeling rather 'puffed up'. As a leader, she had spent time surveying Pony, Rabbit, Bear, Eagle, Beaver and even Snake. What a victory! Her family was still celebrating her success. What she had accomplished seemed rather small compared to the difficult task of dealing with the less fortunate.

"Turtle, I am so sorry. What is to be done? What can we do?"

"Lamb, who are the strong? Should not those with great blessings help those who are not so blessed? Or is it really survival of the fittest for the animal kingdom.
 That is a question you must answer before we talk about any action."

"Isn't it true? Survival of the fittest is almost a mantra."

"This 'mantra' may be a dangerous one for those who cannot afford for you to think that way. You are the leader after all."

"Turtle, sometimes I hate being the leader. It isn't as if I can walk over there, whistle and everyone will signal their deformity or need and I will find an answer! It takes so much from me. I can't sleep. The responsibility overwhelms me. It's difficult! Part of me doesn't want to deal with this. I brought most across. The others can find a leader and cross. And then I am overwhelmed by my selfish nature. How can I leave them there with no effort on my part? This is the conflict in my heart."

"Lamb, these are choices you must make." As for me, I will await you answer.

"Turtle, what about you? You have a reputation of being wise. Can't you deal with them?"

"Them!" Them! What are you saying? Are they a pronoun in your mind?" Regardless of what I do, your decision is yours. I wait for it."

Turtle slowly turned and walked toward the bridge. Her mind was on the opposite side from Lamb's. She needed to think about her responsibility to those who could not cross the bridge without help. Perhaps Lamb had done her job. Was it now hers alone? Or not? Would anyone listen to her? How could she lead? She was used to sitting, watching, judging and sitting quietly feeling 'above it all'. What would happen if she came out and got involved? Would anyone listen? She felt very uncomfortable. And yet, her heart was with the less fortunate.

Turtle was very angry. She was put in this position by Lamb and by the progress of those much stronger than her friends. Bulldozers, trucks, macadam, concrete was manipulated by people for their own purposes. They all had blinders that could not see the living just beyond their machines. How many had already been affected? Some woke in the morning having to scurry to a new place only to move a few short weeks later. Others weren't so lucky. Their nests included the eggs waiting to be born. They were broken and swept away with the dirt. Some were crippled and left to find their way. Sometimes a person would grab the animal and throw it aside. Other times the animal would be held up for exhibit and ended up being thrown away like garbage.

Turtle began to think the way those who had experienced people must feel. Scared. Angry. Ever vigilant. Left Behind. Looking for direction: choices rather than no choice.

Literally, they were the underdog; under the machines, buildings etc. Forced to made choices. No choice a good one.

It did come to Turtle's mind that she could not afford to sit and do nothing if she were to stay. It is as if the bridge was the choice for him also. Choose the bridge; go to the new land; live on.

Choose to stay: forever endangered. It seems like an easy choice. There she was: at the bridge facing her decision. For some reason, it was not an easy one. Was she afraid? Could it be complacency? Could it be that she did not know? She knew she had to get involved. Getting involved was so frustrating. Turtle so wanted to claim the knoll and sit in judgment. There was no turning back. Yes, no turning back but how to move ahead? Now regardless of where she walked, the problem was carried with her. Even if she crossed the bridge, the burden of remembering would be with her. How could Lamb leave them? Didn't she feel the same way: a pull back to this side to continue the crusade of moving every animal to the new land? Turtle waited.

Back Home

Whew! It seemed like weeks rather than an afternoon and morning. Turtle came back across the bridge with an extra load of responsibility. Without realizing Turtle headed back to the knoll. This little hill represented a familiarity for Turtle. She so longed to be there. Stay there. Make pronouncements inside and wait. Was there a new roll? She found herself sitting there, feeling ever so comfortable but not for long! Somehow uneasiness crept into her complacency. The imprint of her less fortunate invaded the peace she once knew.

Turtle hoped that Lamb would return and lead everyone across with great fanfare. She decided to sit on the hill and watch to see if Lamb would save the day.

Eagle had been flying over the bridge and heard the interchange between Turtle and Lamb. Seeing Turtle settle on her imagined throne, Eagle decided to fly down next to her.

"Hey! Turtle" Have you been to the new land? What a sight! I have found so many places on which to perch. I love it!

"Well, yes, I have strolled over. I have even spoken to Lamb. She is so thrilled to see her friends and family in the new land; away from the terror of the people's progress."

"Yes, she is pleased, very pleased."

"Eagle, you fly back and forth over the bridge. What do you see on this side? Your view is so much wider than mine."

Well, there is indeed quite a contrast. On this side, things are changing very quickly. The machines are bigger and bigger, pushing great mounds at one time over and over again day after day. It is incredible to see the destruction of trees. Those machines look like huge monsters in a terrible dream. In comparison, the other side is paradise. There are no metal monsters tearing the earth; leveling the land and leaving it barren. Instead, the trees continue to grow as they have for centuries. Food is plentiful. A natural survival of the fittest is allowed.

"Eagle, do you think there is room for those left behind?" asked Turtle.

"Of course there is space. And there is healing. When there is plentiful food, the disabled can suffer no more fear, eat well and get better."

"How would you go about bringing them to the new land?"

"I can tell you where they are. I don't have any idea of how to persuade them once someone goes to them," answered Eagle.

"You know I have sat on my little hill for all of my life thinking that my job was to sit in judgment of life in the forest. I enjoyed reflecting. Now it seems I am being asked to take action. I am at a loss as to what to do. As you know, I move slowly."

"Slow or not, you are the wise counsel. Others are expecting you to help. That's not the most important question. The real question is, "What is your heart calling you to do?" said Eagle.

"My very soul is telling me to move mountains to save the less fortunate," said Turtle. But what can I do?"

"I don't know. I have told you what I can do."

"I may take you up on that," said Turtle.

"Well, let me know. You will see me in the sky."

No ideas came to Turtle. Perhaps, he was feeling too much: thinking too little. Again, she yearned to be on her promontory reflecting. Slowly, she moved in that direction.

As she moved, she heard a rumbling. Looking up, Turtle was

surprised to see the monster moving toward her space. Fear filled her. She attempted to move quickly but hurry was not part of her being. At that moment she knew that she would not be able to do much for some of the animals. They were gone! How many would be able to cross the bridge?

Moving ever so slowly and with a tear falling, Turtle moved her head inside her own shell. Perhaps in the dark, an idea would form. Perhaps, for the first time, Turtle would find God and he would answer his prayer.

Lamb was having the same feelings as Turtle with one exception. She had seen success. Even though part of her was ready for the challenge. Another side wanted to play the success card. She craved that 'you are great' theme. She had certainly earned it by taking her friends across the bridge. The land was also her reward. Somehow she thought she certainly owned part of it. Each morning she would survey her kingdom. She relished the choice of meadows, the tall trees, the brook at the bottom of the hill. Life was easy.

She wished she had never spoken with Turtle. What went through her mind again and again were those who have been blessed. That truly was a description of her. Blessed to be chosen with leadership, blessed to have the skills needed, blessed to be a significant part of the community. How to get rid of the flu of responsibility in her belly was the pressure placed on her heart and mind? Wasn't it time for someone else to lead? Surely she was not the only leader who could help. Turtle sat on her knoll, his 'high thoughts' piercingly judging the world around him. Maybe it is time for him to get off the high mountain and come to the valley of struggle. Yeah!

Remembering that Turtle was waiting, Lamb crossed over the bridge to give Turtle her reply.

Turtle was waiting.

"Good morning, Lamb. I am so happy to see you."

"I am not sure you will be when I give you my answer", replied Lamb.

"What! You are not going to help?"

"Turtle, I have done my part. I started the journey. It's someone else's time to lead. Maybe it is your turn."

"But Lamb, I am not a leader. I am a philosopher, a discerner: one who gives prophecy."

"What? And how can that be used in the real world of change?" voiced Lamb.

"Well, I describe what is wrong and give prophecy to what will happen. I warn of the coming doom. That's my role. I feel most comfortable doing just that!" explained Turtle.

"And comfort is a reason for inaction?" Lamb replied a bit sarcastically.

"Isn't that why you won't come back? You are feeling comfortable over there with your friends? Your accomplishment is behind you. Now you revel in the aftermath of what you consider to be greatness."

Turtle! Stop it!

Lamb reiterated, "You stop! Stop throwing responsibility to some one else. It belongs to."

Lamb answered his own inner calling, "It belongs to us!"

"Are you telling me I was a part of this problem when I only sat here and never hurt anyone" yelled Turtle.

And then she heard her voice, her inner voice. It wasn't a pleasant one because it brought with it realization. By not saying anything she had caused too much time to pass by. Now there was a crisis. She could no longer look down but across the land.

"What shall we do, Lamb?"

"I don't know. I don't know. What I do realize is that we must do something quickly."

Turtle agreed.

What turtle wanted to do was rush away. Think.

What Lamb wanted was to go back to the land across the bridge.

Neither could.

Turtle could not go into his dark comfortable place inside his shell.
Lamb could not go to the meadow to think.

They had to face each other and make a decision that would have
consequences. One would save the animals; another would leave
them to die.

"Who can help?" said Lamb.

"Everyone", answered Turtle.

"What?"

"Everyone. I mean each animal who was blessed enough to get to
the other side. They must return and bring some animals across to
the new land."

"I had to bring each animal across: one by one. Now you tell me
each animal has to do the same?   asked Turtle.

"Let's pray that the animals will cross back over the bridge to find
their fellow animals," said Lamb. My prayer is that the invisible
force does not return."

"Lamb, you get the animals back to the bridge. I will work with
Eagle to find the homes of animals that need to cross over the
bridge. We will meet at the bridge tomorrow at noon."

"Ok."

At the Bridge

It had been an exciting day. The animals were very willing to come to the bridge and listen. No one promised to cross the bridge.

Turtle had met with Eagle and had a map of places that the animals must visit in order to help loved ones move toward the bridge. One had to admit the two came to the bridge with their tasks completed.

Lamb began, "My dear friends, thank you for coming to the bridge from your havens on this side of the bridge. How blessed you are! Turtle and I are here to tell you that there are animals on the other side. They need to cross the bridge. They need to fight the invisible force. They are in danger more than you because time has passed allowing the machines to encroach further and further toward the bridge. Some animals have been pushed from their homes. They are scared and yet fear the crossing. I am indeed frightened that they will not be able to cross. They are not as healthy as you; they have been left behind because they cannot cross without help. Just as I helped each of you, I am asking you to cross back over the bridge long enough to bring an animal back across with you. Power is in our numbers. What say you to this plan? Turtle and Eagle know where each animal is and will be ready to give direction to each family. The question is whether you will cross over to help or not. The consequences will not be yours but the ones on the other side waiting for one animal to help them cross."

"Ok, line up for your assignments", said Turtle.

"Wait just a minute!" answered Pony. My family is here. I have a responsibility to them. I can't cross the bridge unless I can be assured I will return." Who will guarantee that I will return?"

"That's just it. There is no guarantee. You will have to risk! You are fast and strong. We need you because you are fast and strong.

You can gallop across and return quickly," answered Lamb.

"Well, I am not afraid, bristled Bear. I can cross the bridge."

"Yes, you can find the weak and bring them back across," said Lamb.

"Rabbit, you can scurry across and return quickly bringing the less fortunate with you," said Turtle.

"What about that force? I still remember the force. It scared me," replied Rabbit.

"Do you have enough courage to help those in need?" asked Lamb.

Turtle stepped forward. "Listen, I have been sitting on my hill watching you. I saw your skepticism the first time you tried to cross the bridge. How did you get to the other side? Lamb had the courage to assist you in crossing. We are grateful to her. Now we are asking each of you to find within whatever you need to do the same for your families and friends who are in need. Let's join together, find strength in each other and do the job that we all know must be done. Otherwise, the new dream will be an elitist one."

"Ok, who will be the first to sign up?" asked Turtle.

"I will but I won't go across the bridge. I will go the way I came over," answered Beaver.

"Thank you, Beaver."

"I am looking for people to follow me across the bridge," stated Lamb.

Animals began to move toward Lamb forming an army of helpers.

Soon everyone was in line to cross the bridge and find someone to lead to the new land.

Turtle was overwhelmed with the courage in numbers. He suddenly let out a huge cry.

"Thank you so much! I look forward to a new land that includes the needy. I see a new community where each animal looks beyond their own family to those who need help. And each animal acts upon what they see. In return, their lives will receive great blessings. And just maybe the next time an outside source invades, the community can stand together, hold together and know that no animal needs to be alone. As for me, I see my life changing. I commit to move from my haughty existence. Next time I won't sit there and expound on the world but will get involved using my gifts in a loving, caring way.

Lamb looked at Turtle. We have learned how to stay together forming a caring community. We have defeated the invisible force and in its place we have community.

Tears came from Turtle's eyes. "From disaster to community.

What Lamb Learned

To conquer fear
To seek God's voice
To be on the edge of the wall of change
To push through the walls of emotion

To make choices and learn from the consequences
To be an active listener
To be humble
To love unconditionally

To lead to the promised land
To form community
She is feeling good!
Very good!

Made in the USA
Lexington, KY
25 March 2012